CYCLING TRAINING MADE SIMPLE, SMART, AND SAFE

UNDERSTAND HOW TO CYCLE IN 60 MINUTES

CHRISTIAN HORNER

INTRODUCTION

** Before starting any sport or exercise program it is always advisable to consult a physician first.

Welcome to the world of cycling, your new sport is one that is bred of blood, sweat, tears and fiery European passion. Cycling can be as easy and as hard as you choose to make it and the goal of this book is to provide you with good, sound advice to help you enter the sport in the best, most informed way possible.

Whether you prefer to bounce in and out of rock gardens with some friends on a mountain bike, speed along in a peloton with your super light road machine or just cruise to work on a commuter bike, the sport of cycling is one that can be extremely rewarding. It can also be very humbling, as one day you will feel like no mountain is too big and the next you may find yourself suffering to get to the top of the small hill at the end of the road.

It is a sport that you will learn to love as you figure out its nuances and quirks; it is also never short of humour and drama and comes with an abundance of passion.

You may find it is highly social as you join groups and

make friends and then it will take you on an introspective journey while you cover endless miles on trails and paths with nothing but yourself and your bike to worry about.

Cycling will give you the means and energy to explore some of the most beautiful places in your state, in your country and possibly even the world, if you are fortunate enough. Every once in a while take a moment to reflect on your surroundings and achievements since you started cycling

Starting off with the correct equipment and a responsible training plan will help you enjoy the sport of cycling much sooner than if you were trying to find your way around in the dark.

This EBook is designed to help those new to the sport of cycling get the most out of the sport and their equipment as quickly as possible. Once you are comfortable with your bicycle and your equipment you can begin a training program that if followed consistently, will have you achieving your cycling goals as quickly as possible.

1. THE BIKE

If you are yet to purchase a bike then you need to decide what discipline of cycling appeals to you most right now and what your cycling goals are as this will determine what bicycle and equipment to purchase.

1.1 Commuter Bicycles

The commuter, this is a bike that will be used mostly on tarred roads over short distances in an urban area as a means to get to work, go shopping or the odd social event. The bike of choice is a commuter specific bike designed for maximum comfort and slow to medium speeds. A commuter cyclist in general does not do any training, but simply uses the bicycle to get from one point to the next. Many commuter bicycles include racks or bike bags for transporting items.

1.2 Road Bicycles

Road Bikes are slim, light, aggressive looking bicycles, with narrow wheels and precise components that are all designed to go fast.

Most manufacturers' produce two* categories of road bikes:

- A ride line which is by no means slow, but the geometry of the bike is slightly more relaxed and upright to provide a more comfortable ride. There is often a choice between Composite (Aluminum) or carbon which is generally a lot lighter and stiffer than the Alu. The components would range from entry level to professional.

- The race line of bikes is more aggressive in geometry and less comfortable and not recommended as a first bicycle. These incredibly light bikes are fitted with top-end professional components on a carbon frame and tend to be a lot more expensive than the ride range. This range of bicycles is built with racing in mind.

*Some manufacturers also produce impressive looking bicycles called Time Trial bikes which are intended for Time Trial races or ultra distance triathlons. These machines are designed to be very aerodynamic and fast, but in general do not corner or ascend very well. Unless you are intending to do Ironman distance triathlons or time trial races these should not be considered and are mostly not permitted to be used in regular road races.

1.3 Mountain Bicycles

Mountain biking has become one of the fastest growing sports in the world with several different genres of mountain biking to choose from.

- Downhill mountain biking is fast, highly technical and requires a dual suspension bike with a front fork bearing a minimum of 160mm of *travel. Expect high speeds, large drops and big ramped jumps, you will need full face helmets and body armor. This is a sport for the serious adrenaline junkie.
- Trail and Enduro riding is less technical, but is still not for the faint hearted, the bikes have less front fork travel (120mm – 140mm) but are dual suspension bikes. Normal cycling apparel is appropriate.
- Cross-Country and Marathon cycling are the most popular mountain bike disciplines and hard tail mountain bikes are more popular as they provide a better ride when climbing, but are still responsive on the descents. The front fork will have modest amount of travel of between 80mm – 120mm. This discipline appeals to a much broader spectrum of athletes and there is a larger range of bicycles to choose from. There are also a much larger number of social events and races on offer to take part in.

*Travel is the amount of distance the front fork of a bike can compress, this compression is what takes the majority of the shock when landing a jump or rolling over a large obstacle.

There are literally dozens of brands of mountain bikes on the market and choosing one that suits your budget and chosen discipline can be tricky. Take some time to research the brand you are interested in and take note of the manufacturer's warranty and international presence.

ONE

2. BIKE SETUP

This is an incredibly important part of purchasing a bicycle as the benefit of a good bike setup cannot be underestimated. A poor or incorrect setup can lead to severe discomfort and eventually injury.

The correct size frame sets the basis for a good setup and components of varying size can be built up around this depending on body measurements.

Each bicycle brand has different geometries based on the technology and type of frame that is produced, the good brands almost always have a sizing chart to find the correct fit.

Most cycle shops offer a free basic setup when purchasing a bike that should address the following size factors:

- Crank arm length, this should correspond to your leg length and height; crank arms come in several different lengths with the most popular lengths at 172.5mm and 175mm.

- Check and adjust the seat post height and forward position.
- Check and fit the correct stem length and angle based on your height and body length

Ensure that the setup is done with your cycling shoes as this is critical to obtain the correct position on the bike.

Too often cyclists are sold a frame that is too large, causing the body to over extend and stretch making the experience both uncomfortable and over terrible back pain over long periods of riding. The bike will also feel unresponsive and sluggish.

If a frame is too small, the cyclist will feel cramped and after a short period of riding will experience knee pain and injury.

Once your various measurements have been taken and the correct components fitted your bicycle will feel better, respond better and reduce the potential for injury. Take note of how your body feels on the bike and if you experience discomfort and pain for an extended period of time it is advisable to get the setup checked.

TWO

3. THE EQUIPMENT

You now have the bike and the salesperson is recommending a seemingly endless list of other gadgets and devices, some of which don't seem necessary and some of them aren't, but you will need a few of these to make sure you are equipped for most eventualities when out on the road or trail.

3.1 Helmet

This is the most valuable piece of equipment that you will buy as it could save your life and in many countries you are required by law to wear one when cycling. Don't go cheap on your choice, but you probably also don't need a top of the range model when you start. Aim for mid price range and ask an experienced sales assistance to help get the correct fit. Most good brands have cm/inch measurement on the inside so all you need is a tape measure.

3.2 Multi Tool

This is a tool which you can slip into your back pocket or saddlebag and is invaluable. It should be equipped with several hex keys to fit most bolts on your bike, a screw driver set and many also incorporate a chain link removal tool. Remember to ask for a spare chain link for your specific chain.

3.3 Tubes

It goes without saying that you will eventually get a puncture and spending time trying to fix a puncture is never fun. Take along a spare tube or even two. For those mountain bikers who are using tubeless it is advisable to take a tube along as a big enough hole in the tire won't let the sealant set. Tubeless setups consist of a kit that uses a sealant in the wheel; this sealant reacts to seal a puncture when one occurs. If a puncture is too large the sealant might not be able to seal the hole.

3.4 Pump/CO2 Inflator

It goes without saying if you have a tube you will need to inflate it, many cyclists these days use CO_2 canisters which hold compressed air and used along with a small inflator pumps, up a tire in seconds, if you are going out on a long ride it is advisable to carry a pump too.

3.5 Tire Levers

A good sturdy pair of these will help you take a tire off to get to the punctured tube, and should be considered as a necessity item.

3.6 Water Bottles or Hydration Packs

Sports Physicians advise that you consume around 750ml of fluid for every hour of exercise. Most water bottles come in 500ml to 750ml sizes so get yourself a few as you will probably use two on the bike. Recently the use of non-PET bottles has become popular because of health concerns, but these are slightly more expensive. If you use the standard PET bottles they should be discarded after about six to eight months of use as the plastic degrades.

Hydration packs are very often used in mountain biking as trails often take cyclists into areas that are remote and fresh water is not readily available. Hydration packs are also convenient as they are able to carry more spares, tools and food.

3.7 Lights

The nature of cycling is that the training hours are long and many cyclists still need to balance full time jobs and family time so they often have to resort to early morning or evening training. To train safely in the early morning or after dark a good set of lights is required for the front and rear of the bike. A set of front lights that are specified at 1000 lumens and above will give you plenty of light and the battery packs for these will give you around 3hrs of riding time. Less important on the trails, but very important on the road is a flashing rear light that will make you visible to motorists and other cyclists. Rear lights are not expensive and it is often convenient to have more than one around in case of battery failure.

3.8 Computer/Heart Rate Monitor (HRM)

These devices are useful and vitally important for training. Depending on the brand, the device will display various metrics including distance, time, speed, heart rate and many others. To start training effectively a quality heart rate monitor is critical with many of the newer models fitted with GPS which will give more accurate distance, elevation and other training information.

Training statistics and metrics can be measured on a semi-professional level using power meters. This training tool has become more popular and more affordable. Power meters coupled with heart rate monitors gauge the amount of power that a cyclist is exerting in watts. It is often a more accurate benchmark to train with as heart rate as training can be affected by many variables including stress, lack of sleep and illness. Power meters are readily available at most bicycle shops but unless you are considering some serious racing they are not necessary.

THREE

4. MAINTENANCE

The substantial investment that you have made when buying a bicycle should to be looked after and regular maintenance will increase the longevity of all your components. You need not do it yourself as most cycle shops offer a clean and lube service that costs a few Dollars. Doing the clean and lube yourself once a week will however give you a better idea of how the components work and how you can fix them yourself should you need to.

Mountain bikes need to be maintained regularly as the components are prone to excessive wear and tear due to dust, mud, sand, rocks and generally a much tougher riding environment. A mountain bike that is ridden a few times a week should be washed weekly and if a ride is particularly muddy and dirty a wash after such ride is advisable. Depending on your riding environment, a mountain bike should also have a minor service once every two or three months and a major service every six months, your bike shop will be able to determine which parts are starting to wear and which parts need replacing.

Road bikes require much less maintenance and tend to stay cleaner for longer; unless a ride has been in rainy conditions a road bike can be cleaned once or twice in a month. Service intervals would be determined by your mileage, but a minor service every six months and a major service once a year should keep your road bike running optimally.

Lubrication of the chain will assist in extending the life of your chain and cluster, but do not over lubricate your chain. Chains that have been over lubricated become sticky which allows them to pick up dust and sand particles. This creates a corrosive paste that wears away at your cluster, chain-rings and chain.

The lubricant you choose should be a non-solvent as you do not want to destroy the lubricants your chain was manufactured with. Once you have lubricated your chain take a cloth or paper towel to wipe off any excess lubricant.

When your bicycle is being serviced get your bike shop to check the chain wear, as replacing a chain before it wears too much will prolong the life of your cluster and chain-rings.

High pressure cleaners can be used to wash your bike, but do not take the nozzle too close to any of the bearings on the bike as the high pressure tends to push dirt into the bearings which results in friction and wear.

FOUR

5. CLOTHING

The correct clothing can go a long way to give you a more comfortable and pleasant ride and clothing should be chosen based on your environment and discipline but the basic remain the same, buy and wear what you are comfortable wearing.

5.1 Shorts

The comfort that a good pair of cycling shorts offers cannot be underestimated as this is largest contact point you have with your bike, other contact points are your hands and feet. The chamois in the shorts is the pad that protects the I.T. or sit bones from the saddle and is responsible, along with the saddle, for creating a comfortable riding experience.

Choosing shorts from a well known manufacturer with a high quality chamois is advisable if you are intending on spending long periods on the bike. Poorly fitting shorts with a low quality chamois can cause saddle sores which if become infected can be a serious health risk and are extremely painful. Saddle sores have even been responsible for the withdrawal of many professional cyclists from some of the world's biggest cycle races including the Cape Epic and Tour de France.

Choosing bib shorts over conventional shorts is also advisable as they tend to move less although some cyclists find the shoulder straps on bibs to be uncomfortable. The choice of shorts or bibs will be something that each cyclist needs to choose for themselves and finding the correct chamois may not happen immediately and will come down to skin sensitivity and personal choice.

Hygiene with cycle shorts is incredibly important so it is advisable to wash your shorts after a ride with a good detergent. Many of the top end manufacturers incorporate antibacterial fabrics into the chamois.

5.2 Tops

Cycle tops need to provide UV protection and comfort, should be breathable and wick sweat off the body. Cycle shirts should also be chosen with the local environmental and seasonal conditions in consideration. Clothing manufacturers will produce winter and summer lines of clothing, so purchase these and wear as and when the season change. Windbreakers are light and fold up very small, allowing them to easily be carried in the back pocket of a shirt.

Pockets at the rear of the cycle top are also important as you will need to be able to store food and emergency spares in these.

5.3 Gloves

As another contact point to the bike, your hands will require protection and a decent set of gloves will prevent discomfort and blisters. Short finger gel padded gloves make for a comfortable and cool riding experience. If you are riding off road then a pair of full finger hard wearing gloves is advised to protect your fingers from stones, mud, branches and other objects that might be thrown up from the trails. Good padding on mountain gloves will also help absorb shock waves from the handlebars on rough terrain.

5.4 Shoes

This is your third contact point and possibly the most important as this where the driving force is. Your foot position on the pedal determines your body position on the bike, so it is vital that your bike setup is done with your cycle shoes.

Road shoes differ to mountain bike shoes and are easily distinguishable as road shoes have a smooth plastic or carbon sole, mountain bike shoes however have studded or gripped soles.

There are dozens of shoe brands to choose from with very disparate pricing and quality. Finding the right shoe will come down to your foot type and shape, fashion and personal choice. Try a couple of shoes on before buying to find the most comfortable fit as you will be spending a lot of time wearing these.

5.5 Weather Gear

Appropriate kit to suit the weather conditions in your area is important and manufacturers produce winter range and also wet weather gear. A gilet or windbreaker is a convenient and light piece of clothing that will keep the wind off your chest and very often has a mesh or breathable back to keep you cool.

A light rain jacket is important as it will keep you dry and warm; these jackets are breathable and fold up small so they are convenient to put in a back pocket. If you are unsure about the weather then rather pack one of these as riding when wet can become unpleasant and cold.

Shoe covers made from lycra or neoprene keep your feet

warm in cold conditions with waterproof booties providing a dry alternative in wet conditions.

5.6 Eyewear

A good pair of sunglasses is essential for protection from the sun and stray objects. Small stones, dust and glass litter the roads and these can often be thrown up from the road by the wheel in front of you and cause irritation or injury.

Trails are dusty and loaded with small objects that are often thrown up in the face and a good pair of sunglasses will offer priceless protection.

Protect your eyes in the dark by using a set of clear or low light lenses.

FIVE

6. SAFETY

Once you have firmly secured your helmet to your head and get out onto the road or trail there are a few basics that should be followed to ensure your cycle is as safe and pleasant as possible.

Before you leave on your ride use the resources around you to check the weather so you can plan your ride and gear accordingly as conditions can change very quickly. The windguru.cz website is reliable and accurate.

If possible, plan your route beforehand, this will not only assist you to prepare equipment and clothing accordingly, but gives you the opportunity to let others know where you intend to ride and how long you intend to ride for. Anything can happen out on the roads or trails and if emergency services have a reference point to search from it could save your life.

Take a mobile phone along with you on the ride, it is a convenient emergency tool and there are many cheap disposable cell phones on the market if you don't want to take your expensive smartphone.

Always be aware of your surroundings, take note of road signs or warnings and be aware of changing weather conditions.

Ride within your ability, don't wake up in the morning and set out on a 160km ride if you have never completed more than 80 km's before.

When out on public roads you are obliged to obey general road rules unless it is otherwise indicated.

It is a global problem that many cyclists tend not to obey traffic lights or stop signs, these signals and signs are there for your safety and should be obeyed at all times. It is unlikely that small regional road races will have full road closure, but many of these races will have marshals to assist with traffic, but normal traffic laws and regulations should be adhered to unless a race official or traffic officer indicates otherwise.

Most road laws advise cyclists to try ride as close to the side of the road as possible(right hand side in US and Europe, left hand side in UK, Southern Africa and some Asian regions) and riding in the direction of the traffic. Never ride into oncoming traffic this is considered extremely dangerous.

Visibility aids such as a rear facing red flashing light will help increase your visibility to traffic coming up from behind, LED lights on the front of your bike will announce your presence on the road clearly. When riding in the dark wear bright or reflective clothing to make yourself more visible to traffic.

Always try and anticipate what a driver is going to do, for instance, if you are approaching an intersection where a car is waiting to enter the road look at the driver and try to make eye contact. Most times you will be able to see if the driver has observed you or if they are about to make a move.

Riding in groups is not always possible, but if you are able to ride with a group then it is advisable, a large group is more visible to motorists and in general groups are less vulnerable than a single rider.

SIX

7. CYCLING LAWS

ALWAYS OBEY THE LAW!

Many countries and often provinces or states will have their own set of cycling laws governing how cyclists are required to behave on the road and sometimes on trails.

In many regions it is law that cyclist must wear helmets and often IPod's or music players are banned for use when cycling on public roads.

More often than not, bicycles are considered as vehicles when using public roads and as such normal traffic laws apply to cyclist. Road markings and signs should be obeyed and common sense should used at all times.

If you are unsure of the laws in your area then do some research online or ask around at your local bike shop for advice.

SEVEN

8. CYCLING CLUBS

Joining a local cycling club is the easiest way to meet like-minded people, learn more about the sport in general and how it operates in your region. Cycle clubs will organize group rides, social events and workshops for various cycling related topics. Many clubs are also associated with a cycle retailer and here you will be able to pick up good advice and find a good bike mechanic.

EIGHT

9. SKILLS

Basic bike handling skills are gained by virtue of spending time on the bike, but there are many other skills that should be practiced by both road cyclists and mountain bikers.

Road cycling has far less skills to master, but are no less important than those used on the trail.

Cornering is a great skill to master as you descend fast winding roads and when racing this skill can gain you a substantial advantage.

The first step to cornering is head position, look where you are intending to go and try not brake while you are in the corner. Take the corner from the widest position possible and cut in towards the apex of the turn, at this point you should be looking at the exit which should be at the widest possible point much like the starting point. It is also important to pedal out of the corner as soon as you can without compromising the turn.

Riding in a peloton is also a skill that is important both from a racing strategy point of view, but also for safety. The ability to ride comfortably within a peloton and be able to anticipate its behavior and relax is one that can only be gained by riding in groups. Many road cyclists find themselves in the middle of a group in their first few races and become nervous and claustrophobic causing them to act dangerously and irrationally which in most cases leads to an accident. Training with a group will help you learn how pelotons work as they slow on rises and accelerate in dips and spread out on descents before bunching up again on climbs.

A skill that is best to learn quickly is handling a bike with one hand, you will need this skill to eat and drink on the bike. When you first start cycling find a quiet road where you can practice taking your bottle out of the bottle cage, drinking and then returning it. Also work at peeling a banana or unwrapping your energy bar while pedaling.

Mountain bike skills are much different and require a lot of time and practice to master, but when you get these skills right your ride will become faster and much more enjoyable.

As with road cycling and cornering, a cyclist should look at where they intend to go, but many cyclists tend to look at the object in their path that they are trying to avoid. Rather look at the path around the object and you will successfully roll past it.

Look ahead of you and not at the ground just in front of your wheel as this will give you time to adjust your body weight and prepare your bike for what you are approaching.

Control is everything on a mountain bike and sitting glued to your saddle while riding down a trail will only slow you down and eventually bounce you out of your seat and off the bike. Stand up on the pedals, lean forward keeping your centre of gravity in the middle of the bike. Once you have this position on the bike you will have the correct balance and positioning to move the bike around underneath you, to hop over ditches, lean into bermed corners or lift the front wheel over obstacles.

Once you hit the hills and flatter trails you can sit again, but keeping your weight centered you will get the correct traction and control from both the front and back wheels.

Becoming familiar with your gears will help you make the correct selections when you need to. There is nothing worse that coming out of dip into a sharp rise and realizing that you are in the wrong gear. Anticipating what gear you need to be in on the trails is one that each cyclist learns over time as they become familiar with both gear ratios and their own strengths.

Speed is your friend, this sometimes seems counterintuitive, but as you become more skilled you will realize that the more speed that is carried into technical paths, rock gardens and corners the easier you will roll over objects, be pushed into the correct lines or ride over drops that look intimidating when riding at low speed. This said each cyclist needs to be aware of their own limitations and ride responsibly within their limits.

If you are not comfortable riding a technical descent or drop off then stop, get off the bike and evaluate the route that you are attempting and watch a more skilled cyclist ride the route so you can pick up what lines should be taken. Walk the section and then attempt once you have the confidence.

There is no shame in riding away from a technically difficult route to return another day once your skills and confidence have improved. Many highly skilled riders will evaluate a difficult route several times before attempting it.

NINE

10. ETIQUETTE

There is an unwritten code of conduct that cyclists adhere to and getting to know the basics will help you read what is happening on the road around you, what your fellow cyclists are doing and make your ride much safer.

Try not to make sudden unpredictable moves on the bike particularly when riding in a bunch as this is likely to cause the riders behind you to react and the riders behind them with a potentially nasty domino effect.

Let riders know what is coming up in the road, many cyclist do this by slapping the side of their hip and then pointing down to the side where the object is or even using a sweeping motion with the hand to show the rider behind to move in behind as there is a larger object like a parked car coming up. Hand gestures should also be used if you intend turn, if you are slowing or intending to stop then put your hand out behind you with your palm facing back.

Informative verbal instructions can also be given but keep them simple and brief.

Hole! would indicate that there is a hole in the road ahead.

Car Back! informs riders that there is a car approaching from behind and that they should keep a bit closer to the side of the road.

Passing! this indicates to riders that you are intending to pass.

As you increase your heart rate and then reduce it, then increase it again you will find that mucus and spit will gather in your nose and mouth which you will want to expel. When doing so move safely to one side and ensure that no cyclists are directly behind you when getting rid of these body fluids.

Do not litter, throwing a gel sachet or wrapper from a bar on the ground is completely unacceptable for a cyclist. Put any litter you have in your back pocket and discard it when your ride is done.

Over and above these basics, common courtesy will keep you in good stead with your fellow riders.

TEN

11. TRAINING

There are a few reasons cyclists start looking for a training program and no matter your reason the goal needs to be achievable and realistic, for instance setting out as beginner to win an ultra distance race in six months is more than likely not going to happen.

T.I.T.S, Time In The Saddle is where the basics to any program should start. This is your base and coupled with consistency will have your fitness and endurance increasing in a short period of time.

11.1 Heart Rate

Once a good base has been established you can add more structure into your training. To benefit from a structured plan you will need to determine your maximum heart rate (HR), a loose gauge for this is to take 220 and subtract your age. 220 – 30 years old = 190bpm.

The 220 number is a general guideline used by health professionals to get a rough gauge of an individual's max HR. It is by no means highly accurate.

The following are some very basic techniques that are

easy to follow and with some consistency will increase your fitness and strength in very little time.

11.2 HILLS

On a particular ride of 50 km's choose a route that has as many hills as possible, finding a comfortable climbing position and rhythm is the goal.

11.3 Hill Repeats

Find a reasonably hard hill that is fairly long and is fairly quiet. Start with four repeats of four minutes and recover as you ride back down to the start of the hill. After three weeks, up the interval to five minutes with the same repetitions. After another two weeks keep the interval at five minutes, but add an additional repeat. Continue building up until you reach six by six minute intervals and the buildup will look as follows.

4 min x 4 repeats, 4 min recovery
5 min x 4 repeats, 4 min recovery
5 min x 5 repeats, 4 min recovery
6 min x 5 repeats, 4 min recovery
6 min x 6 repeats, 4 min recovery

Once you have reached the 6 min x 6 repeat mark you can use this as your standard weekly interval session, but as you get stronger try find a steeper hill for the repeats.

11.4 LACTIC THRESHOLD **Intervals (LT)**

Lactate is produced every time you exercise and while you maintain moderate levels of exercise your blood flushes the lactate from your system. When you increase your level of effort more lactate is produced to a point where more is being produced than your body is able to flush. This is your lactic threshold.

Determining LT levels can be done in two ways, the first is a scientific method where your blood is tested during exhaustive testing in a laboratory, this method is expensive and out of reach of most athletes.

A field test can also used to help determine your LT level with a time-trial.

You need to find a flattish route of about 5km with clear start and stop points. Do a warm up ride for 30 minutes. When you get to the start you will need to go as hard as you can for the route, you will need your HR equipment to record this session as lap1. Once you have completed the time trial turn around and take a slow ride back to the start and repeat again recording the next session as lap2.

Your LT threshold will be the average heart rate of the two sessions. This number is the heart rate that you will need to maintain during your LT sessions.

Once your LT levels have been determined, you can mix up a series of 2 – 4 intervals at LT Threshold depending on the length. Starting off, you should use shorter intervals with longer recovery. Some great LT workouts can look like this, but always start with a minimum 30 minute warm-up.

4x 6min LT, 4min recovery
4x 10min LT, 5 min recovery
3x 15min LT, 5 min recovery
2x 20min LT, 10 min recovery

Once your LT intervals are done a cycle of minimum 30 minutes at an easy effort is advised.

11.5 Indoor Training

Riding in winter is often difficult or might not be possible at all; so many cyclists are relegated to indoor trainers or spinning bicycles. Indoor trainers turn your bicycle into a stationary trainer; a flywheel provides resistance to the back wheel and the resistance can be changed during the exercise session. Spinning bikes also provide a great indoor workout. The use of indoor trainers and spin bikes is not very exciting, but they do provide a unique workout as the effort exerted is constant as there are no long descents to freewheel and rest.

Spin Bike or Indoor trainer Tempo ride, do a comfortable warm up for 15 minutes, at the 15 minute mark take your heart rate up to 75% of your maximum and sustain this rate for 30 minutes and then finish off with a comfortable 15 minute warm down. As you become fitter the sustained effort portion of this session should be increased.

15 min warm up, 30 min @75%, 15min warm down
15 min warm up, 45 min @75%, 15min warm down
15 min warm up, 60 min @75%, 15 min warm down

Hill training can be substituted on the trainer using heart rate intervals on the indoor trainer.

Start with a warm up of 10 minutes easy, then for 3 minutes take your HR up to 75%, for an additional 2 minutes you will need to pick up the HR to 85%. And then recover for 5 minutes. Repeat this four to six times.

10min warm up - 3 min @75%, 2 min @85%, rest 5min (repeat x 4) warm down 10min.

Note that warm down and recovery should be at little to no exertion, but the legs need to keep turning over.

11.6 CROSS TRAINING

Cycling is a non impact sport and protracted periods (12 months and more) of cycle focus training can lead to a decrease in bone density. Adding an impact sport to your training program can not only have health benefits to your skeletal structure, but also helps to build your strength.

11.7 CORE STRENGTHENING

Our core muscles provide balance and support for all our limbs and good core strength provides a base for your power and speed training to build around. Two core sessions a week will drastically improve overall strength and balance and should take no more the 30 minutes per session.

Follow a short program with some of the below techniques:

Bridge, lying on the floor on your stomach lift yourself onto your elbows and toes keeping the body as straight as possible, hold for 20 – 30 seconds and then rest before repeating 6 times.

Crunches, lie on your back as you would to do a sit-up but raise your shoulders around 4 inches off the ground ensuring that your core is engaged repeating 4x 20 crunches.

Push-ups, almost everybody knows push-ups but concentrate on form while you do them. Start with 4x 10 push-ups and increase repetitions as you become stronger.

Four Post, this is a non-strenuous exercise but engages the core to create stability and balance. Sitting on gym ball with your back straight tilt the hips forward, backwards, to the right and then left. Repeat 15 times.

These are just a few quick exercises that can help build core strength, a gym instructor will be able to advise you on a more advanced routine.

Once again it should be stressed that these training techniques should only be used once a physician has been consulted and confirmed that the athlete is safe to attempt these.

Consulting a sports trainer is always advisable as they are equipped to advise you on a program that will suit your goals, your environment and lifestyle. Sports trainers will also be able to put you in contact with like minded cyclists and training groups in your area.

Group riding is a great way to train as the sport becomes a bit more social and often training goals are reached without the individual noticing, for instance a 100 km weekend cycle is often much less daunting if done with several other athletes rather than as a solo effort. Often friendly competitiveness is created within a group as rider's race to the top of a hill or try pull away from the group; these small races with a group can have great benefit to fitness on the bike.

11.8 Recovery

Recovery is the most neglected part of training and has a critical part to play in an effective training program. Many training programs are broken down in four week blocks with the fourth week scheduled as a recovery or rest week. A rest week does not mean a week of no training, but rather a week where the hours and intensity are reduced. A cyclist whose previous week had totaled 15 hours would then drop to around 5 to 8 hours of easy training. This rest or recovery week is scheduled so the body has time to recover and heal.

Remember that intense training is breaking down old muscle to build new stronger muscle and you body needs to repair this.

ELEVEN

12. RACING

Riding your bike is a great way to get fit, but there is so much more to cycling, couple the beauty of the mountain trails or endless roads with strategy, adrenaline and the desire beat the rider next to you over the finish line, now you're racing.

12.1 Why Race?

Racing brings a whole new dimension to the sport where pushing your fitness and ability become a personal crusade. Training for a race fuels a new enthusiasm and motivation that will drive you to cycle faster and further.

Everyone's reason for racing is as different to the bike they ride, but some of the more common reasons include:

- Lifestyle - many cyclists start racing because the lifestyle is one that attracts fit healthy individuals and families. The people choose to surround themselves with people of similar interests.

- Sport for the family – There are very few sports where whole families can enter the same competitive event, fun rides or races let all ages and genders participate together.
- Healthy Competition – humans are competitive by nature and challenging a friend or colleague creates a healthy competitive environment.
- Racing Snakes – Occasionally a casual race participant may find they have a natural talent for the sport and take up racing at an age group or semi-professional level.
- For the love – Some cyclists are so passionate about the sport that they want to participate any which way they can.
- The Challenge – many cyclist race because the race is simply there. It is a way for individuals to challenge the bodies and minds.

The easiest way to start racing is to contact your local cycling administrative body, cyclists are normally required to register with the authority to enter races or can often pay a day license. These licenses are necessary as many of the cycling bodies will provide registration services, safety personnel and referees to local races to ensure that safety and racing regulations are adhered to. Often local authorities require that sporting events and the athletes are licensed to the sport governing body before they are able to assist and issue permits.

This fee is normally a small annual fee which is worth paying and will often include club or regional association and benefits.

12.2 Race Preparation

Once a race diary has been consulted, a race should be

chosen that is realistic in distance and difficulty and should also allow for enough training time. Novice riders should work on a minimum of an eight week training plan that includes a taper (rest) period which should be the two weeks leading up to the race.

12.3 An example of a simple 8 week plan for an 80km race.

Mon	50km easy ride
Tues	Cross train/Gym
Wed	LT Session 30min warm-up, 4x6min, 4 min recovery
Thurs	
Fri	50km easy ride
Sat	15km recovery ride
Sun	
Week 1	

WEEK 2

REST

30 minute warm-up 4x4 minute hill repeats
Cross train/Gym
50km easy ride

60km ride
15km recovery ride

WEEK 3
REST

50km easy ride
Cross train/Gym
30min warm-up, 4 x 6 min LT

70km ride
30km ride

Week 4
rest
30km easy ride
Cross train/Gym
40km easy ride

40km easy ride

WEEK 5

REST

30 minute warm-up 4x5 minute hill repeats
Cross train/Gym
50km hilly route

60km ride
15km recovery ride

WEEK 6

REST

30 minute warm-up 4x5 minute hill repeats
Cross train/Gym
50km easy ride

90km ride
15km recovery ride

WEEK 7
REST

40 km hilly route
Cross train/Gym
30min warm-up, 4 x 8 min LT

70km ride
15km recovery ride
Week 8
rest
30km easy ride

20km easy ride

10km easy ride
Race Day!

Race preparation should start the week before the race and your checklist should include:

1. Your bicycle should go for a minor service(at minimum a clean, lube and gear check)

2. Check the weather forecast local to the race and take clothing to suit the conditions.
3. Pack your race bag with your kit, helmet, gloves and shoes, recheck this a couple of times
4. Nutrition, make sure you have enough of your regular sports drink, energy bars, bananas etc
5. Check the route, many race organizers put the route map up on-line, go over the route maps and descriptions.
6. Check the venue; make sure you know beforehand how to get to the start and how long it will take to get there. Plan to be at the race venue an hour before the start as this will give you enough time to kit up, go to the bathroom and so on. You may also be required to pre-register for your race number.
7. Do a short warm up; starting a race on cold legs is not great. If you can arrive 20 minutes earlier this should give you sufficient time for a quick warm up ride

Remember to have fun, the race is your reward for the training that you have done.

TWELVE

13. INJURY

The unfortunate side effect of many sports, particularly endurance sports like cycling, is that muscles, tendons and joints become stressed and it is almost guaranteed that you will experience an injury of some sort during your training or racing. How and when you identify the cause and symptoms determines how bad the injury gets, how soon you are able to treat it and how quickly you can recover.

Prevention is always better cure and there are a few activities that can be used in your general routine which can have a decided influence with injury prevention.

13.1 Stretching

Stretching is the simplest method to maintain muscular and tendon flexibility and should not be limited to the legs only. Stretching arms, neck and shoulder muscles will help loosen up the back and hips which will then assist the range of motion in your legs. Ankle, calf and hamstring stretches will release muscle tension throughout the legs.

Treating the fascia in your lower legs can also benefit

you quadriceps and hamstrings; rolling a tennis ball under your foot from front to back will release the fascia.

To stretch the calf and Achilles, use the second step of a stair case, put the ball of your foot on the edge of the step and push the heel down, use your elbow to push down on your quad to push the heel further down. Hold for 20 seconds and change the leg. Repeat 6 times.

Hamstring stretches are as simple as sitting on the floor with your legs out in front of you, bending at the waist try and touch your toes without bending your legs. Go as far as you comfortably can and hold this for 10 seconds, release and repeat four times.

Hips stretches can help release back or lumbar tightness and pain. On an exercise matt get into the push up position and bring you right foot up to the outside of your right hand, looking forward with your head up drop your hips toward the matt. Repeat this stretch 5 times on each side.

13.2 Massage

Massage Therapy can assist with injury prevention, injury detection and muscle release. Having a regular massage with a registered sport massage therapist will help release muscle tension and flush the muscles of residual lactate from intense training. An experienced massage therapist will also be able to pick up on stiffness and tension that could lead to injury and prescribe a course of action.

If a recurring pain is experienced in the same area over a number of rides then it is likely that an injury has occurred and should be treated or at least looked at by a physician or physiotherapist.

13.3 Common Injuries

Achilles Tendonitis – Pain and inflammation of the Achilles.

Patellar Tendonitis – Pain and inflammation below and around the knee.

ITB Pain – Pain on the outside of the leg and knee into the calf

Back and Neck Pain – pain in the lumbar area, shoulders and neck.

For a beginner cyclist many of these aches and pains play a part in body adjustment and building strength, however if the pain persists for more than a week a physician should be consulted.

THIRTEEN

14. HYDRATION & NUTRITION
14.1 Fluids and Electrolytes

While on the bike it is important to stay hydrated and replenish the fluid and minerals that are sweated out during exercise. Cyclists often forget to drink while on the bike, so it is important to get into a habit of drinking every 15 minutes.

For the most part a bottle of plain water for any ride or exercise session under 60 minutes will be sufficient, but as you start going longer and further you will need to start putting a bit more back into your body.

An electrolyte replacement drink will help replenish what you lose and there are hundreds of brands on the market today to choose from, each of these advertising the benefits of using their product.

It is going to be trial and error to find out which specific brand works for you, but start out with a reputable brand such as Hammer, USN, PowerBar, Enervit, High 5, GU, 32GI to name a few. Once you have chosen a brand you will learn quickly enough if the product does or does not work for you and if it agrees with your stomach.

14.2 FOOD **on the Bike**

Filling your bottle with an electrolyte or carbohydrate drink is the first step and if you are looking at putting in some large distances on the bike then food intake will become necessary. Many cyclists take along bananas or sandwiches and then still have stock of sports bars and gels. This again is something you will need to determine over a period of time until you find out what works best for you.

If you are racing then use the nutrition strategy that that you have used when training, this way you will not have any unpleasant surprises during a race with an irritable gut or nausea. Gels are often used during racing which provides a high energy boosts to your system, but in general these spikes are short lived and the gels are intended for this type of use. Never try a gel or any type of nutrition for the first time during a race as you never know how your body will react.

FOURTEEN

15. Shaving your Legs

Probably the most asked question in the history of cycling must be "why do cyclists shave their legs" and there is more than one answer to this question.

For professional and semi-professional cyclists road rash or grazing from a fall is all part of the sport, now add the additional discomfort of cleaning wounds that have hair mixed in and it becomes quite ugly. Many cyclists get regular massage therapy to assist with recovery and injury rehabilitation, continuous massage with hairy legs becomes unpleasant for both the athlete and the massage therapist.

Cycling might also be a little vain and there is also no doubt that a well toned pair of legs looks great, shaving or waxing your legs accentuates the muscle tone.

So whether you decide to shave or wax or keep your legs natural there is an element of cycling culture that has a part to play here and clean shaven muscular legs are part of the sport and identify you as a cyclist.

. . .

16. **The Finish Line**

There are far too many training techniques, cycling pointers tips and tricks to mention into a singular book. The basics that I have covered in this guide will help you ride safely, train hard and race well. Your cycling journey is just beginning and you will never stop learning as cycling is a dynamic sport that is changing year on year as new technologies are uncovered and training techniques introduced.

It is almost certain you will make new friends, meet old ones, race furiously against a stranger and all the while create a bond with a man made machine that defies logic.

No matter where you find yourself and no matter what cycling discipline you choose, take a moment or rather take two and just .... enjoy the ride

www.ingramcontent.com/pod-product-compliance
Lightning Source LLC
Chambersburg PA
CBHW052125110526
44592CB00013B/1748